T0328497

DARK HORSE

DARK HORSE

poems by

Michèle Betty

People! Read Poetry

Dark Horse

Dryad Press (Pty) Ltd
Postnet Suite 281, Private Bag X16, Constantia, 7848,
Cape Town, South Africa
www.dryadpress.co.za/business@dryadpress.co.za

Cover design & typography: Stephen Symons
Copy Editor: Helena Janisch
Cover Image: "Mondays" by Elize de Beer
2019, Sumi ink drawing on Munken pure 29.7cm x 42cm
Set in 9.5/14pt Palatino Linotype

First published in Cape Town by Dryad Press (Pty) Ltd, 2022

ISBN 978-1-990983-28-3 (Print)
ISBN 978-1-990983-29-0 (Electronic)

Visit www.dryadpress.co.za to read more about all our books and to buy them.
You will also find features, links to author interviews and news of author
events. Follow our social media platforms on Instagram and Facebook
to be the first to hear about our new releases.

Dryad Press is supported by the Government of South Africa through the
National Arts Council of South Africa (an agency of the Department of Arts &
Culture), whose assistance is gratefully acknowledged.

for my Mother

CONTENTS

III *Verbatim*

We too,
the more or less just, I feel fall asleep
dreamless forever while the worlds hurl out.
Rest may be your ultimate gift.

– John Berryman, 'Eleven Addresses to the Lord'

Premonition

Last night a creature crossed my path
its muscles lion-taut,
skin grey and rhino-thick beneath
teeth bared in dimmest light.

It did not look me in the eye
but flicked its head, annoyed —
loitered ahead to skulk before
a drawbridge in the void.

I

Verso

Forsake me not when my wild hours come;
Grant me sleep nightly, grace soften my dreams

– John Berryman, 'Eleven Addresses to the Lord'

L'Infra-Ordinaire

You've remembered my life for me
– Jeanne Viall, 'Playful and Poetic'

I remember on the West Rand, pink proteas growing wild and in bloom on the *koppie* outside our house

I remember the filtered sunlight in the sunroom the morning mother carefully ironed the white crêpe of my First Holy Communion dress

I remember my fingers dripping water as I rolled raw rice and lamb mince into veined grape leaves the shape of my hands

I remember sitting at the kitchen table watching mother scoop out pips and pulp from the inside of marrows to make *koosa*

I remember when Joanna told me she could not sit on the park bench because she was black not brown

I remember every Saturday, my father marking the newspaper with a pencil to prepare his bets for the races that afternoon

I remember the noise when the police raided the staff quarters in our road to check that Joanna and people like Joanna had their pass books

I remember the mix of salt and flour on my fingers as I turned soft dough around little balls of meat to make 'caps' for *shis barak*

I remember dropping trays of 'caps' one by one into a swirling pot of simmering mint-scented yogurt, mixed with garlic and butter, and my mother's exclamation, *sahtein*, when I dished up my second helping

I remember sitting on the kitchen counter and mother, with her arm around my waist, making me warm, sweet Five Roses with the tea bags from the evening before

I remember when Joanna knelt on the carpet, looked in my eyes and told me she had to leave to go home

I remember my parents and our *Inglese* neighbours, the Murrays, talking and talking about the bright light of the unidentified flying object that hovered in the sky at dusk for over an hour above our house

I remember listening quietly to my father and uncles whispering of how some years ago, in the 1960s, the Lebanese couldn't own property in Johannesburg because they were not classified as white

I remember the lines of white iceberg roses planted alongside a dusty sand road in a place called Sandton for the opening of the fancy new Maronite Catholic Church, which had been relocated from Fordsburg

I remember the refracted light spilling from the stained-glass windows in the Rosebank Catholic Church, the cool air from the vaulted ceilings, and me peering over the top of the pews trying to memorise the *I Believe*

I remember sitting cross-legged in front of the Telefunken watching Neil Armstrong step onto the moon and my father saying how the Russians must be going crazy

I remember telling my parents that the most popular girl in Grade One was given two rand for the tuckshop not twenty cents

I remember the brown square cardboard suitcase with gold-coloured latches that my *sittoo* and *jiddoo* proudly bought me before I started Grade One

I remember my brother and sister and me travelling around Johannesburg sitting in the boot of my mother's bright yellow Volkswagen beetle

I remember hearing that my mother was 15 when she met my father and 19 when they married

I remember the ash floating in the night air as the flames of the fire that scoured the *koppie* reached right up to our patch of back lawn

I remember using a hosepipe to soak an arc the shape of a sickle moon around the perimeter of the lawn to protect us from the flames

I remember my father sitting around a smoky dining room table with his Sunday night card school playing *Klaberjass*

I remember mother and me serving platters of cheese & tomato sandwiches and whisky and clearing away ashtrays piled with cigarette butts

I remember large family lunches with uncles, aunts, cousins and the parish priest; children running amok all over the house and endless bowls of *meze*

I remember when my mother told me that *sittoo* and *jiddoo* couldn't visit anymore because there was a car accident

I remember that my mother, unable to sleep, was reading 'Thanatopsis' in the middle of the night when she received the call about that accident

I remember learning that the first time my mother had to loan money from her father to pay my father's gambling debts was three months after they married

Collecting Coals

My *sittoo* had an Aga.
Not a modern, sleek
brushed-steel one
but the old-fashioned kind,
cream enamel and cast iron,
four ominous doors
to be wedged open carefully,
with downturned sickle-moon handles
and the stove loaded on one side
with hot coals to build a fire.
Whenever *sittoo* heard
the rumble of the steam train
from her kitchen window,
you, my father, a waif of a boy,
were dispatched down the tracks
that passed your front door.
With one or more of your
six older brothers
dragging you in tow,
you ran barefoot and stumbling
shirt tails flailing
in the winter wind
under a grey-white sky,
to scoop up the remnants of coal
flung carelessly
by the train in its wake.

Habibe

My father, Christopher, was the youngest
of nine children and his mother's secret
favourite. *Habibe*, she would call him.
Habibe. A curly mop of brown hair,
he was the one with cerulean eyes.
Chrissy, they would call out to him, *Chrissy*.
To prove they knew the secret of mother's
favouritism, his brothers locked Chrissy
in dark cupboards. To start, he would first bang
and bang on the doors, then whimper and twitch
for help: but eventually, he could
only wait in terror for brother James
to take pity, and loose him from the bonds
of a deathly darkness that would blind him.

Talisman

On cliffs that nestle high above
the house, while mom lies still asleep,
we children climb the path with Dad.

From stone to stone, a hop and skip,
the wind a breeze, the morning dew
wet on grass wedged between the rocks.

And everywhere—oversized pink
proteas—their blooms cupped in tough
abundant leaves, emerging wild.

You may not pick them, Dad always
would say. *You cannot remove from
the earth, what you cannot return.*

These days, alone on mountain sides,
I walk among the wildflowers
and rub stems of yellow-centred

Synacarpha circled by white
petals thin as tracing paper:
talisman and Solomon's Seal,

nestled between my fingertips.

Stem Cell Sadness

My bones hold a stillness, the far
Fields melt my heart
– Sylvia Plath, 'Sheep in Fog'

My father was a stem cell donor.
Blood drawn from one arm,
then stem cells from his bone marrow

filtered and separated to a bag,
the blood returned to his other arm—
a one in one hundred thousand match.

On Saturday afternoons, stoic and steady,
he would leave the house for hours,
to return, subdued and pasty-faced.

We made hot tea and biscuit butter
sandwiches to cheer him. But he was always
sad for the slip of a boy, waiting to replace

his bone marrow with that of a stranger.

Fey

Each year in April, at Easter,
my family journeyed; a saga
along the N3 to Durban
for a holiday spent at sea.

We settled high above a hill
where cobbled pathways slope and roam
to the warm ocean; plucked pearl shells;
waited to douse our toes in foam.

My brother, sister and I swam
for hours in the clear rock pools,
playing make-believe, lost in dream.
It was here, the fishing boats beached,

bearing all sorts of bits and bobs—
a seal; a shark's head; dead dolphins
trapped inadvertently in nets.
With hindsight, I often wonder:

did those nets and old boats save us
from imminent, lurking danger,
or were they a sign—an omen—
of the calamity to come?

Leaning Out to Touch Sky

When I was just a child, I loved to climb
from the ground of our low-rise
apartment building up to the roof.
I walked along a stone pathway,
crept down a corridor, turned
the corner, climbing the cement
stairwell. Up, floor after floor, I walked,
my hand outstretched to stroke the wall
until I could go no further. Then
I switched to the narrow ladder
hugging the outside walls, climbing
up on wobbly rungs.
When I reached the very top,
I pulled myself over the gap
between parapet and railing
then scrambled onto black roof tiles
listening to the *clip clop* of the slate
wiggling as I walked.
I climbed as far as I dared.
Sat with knees to chest, my arms
around my shins, cheek to knees
leaning out, tipping backwards
with only the sky and air above me,
the birds in the trees below — my home
now fading from view. It was
Mrs de Santos who spoiled it all
complaining to my parents about
the nuisance and noise of clacking tiles

—so I was forbidden to
go back for fear the nosy neighbour
might raise the alarm again.

In the White of the Year

In the 80s and 90s,
brown-veined white butterflies
migrated in millions to the Highveld.
Lying on the grass, peering
through slanted light at clouds
of furry white-winged creatures,
my cousin and I built butterfly hospitals—
makeshift homes for the wounded.

To catch the nimble creatures,
we ran in circles, amok, clutching
at them, closed our fists, shook and shook
until they tumbled out dazed, to be plopped
onto cottonwool tucked hastily inside
a shoebox, the lid slammed shut.
Sometimes we smashed them with rocks.
Sometimes we put dead ones in.

Scientists said they were migrating
from the Kalahari to Madagascar,
but fell into the sea at Mozambique,
never reaching their destination.
But sangomas whispered
the butterflies were our human ancestors;
the pure in heart; angels bringing
grace to the suffering.

A Sordid State

*If only you knew how fully I myself comprehend the sordidness of
my present state.*
— Fyodor Dostoevsky, *The Gambler*

On a chilly evening in July, my father
walks from the gaming tables, along
gravel pathways flanked by fake
grass, to the *rondawel* where Norman
stays: childhood friend, soul- mate,
he bangs on the door— it's after
midnight at a seedy casino, his
pockets turned out. *Norman!*
he yells, *Norman! Give me my
money, I want it now.* But
Norman is wise to this
weakness. While my father,
flush and broke, argues,
cajoles, refuses to leave,
Norman calls security
heavyweight buffoons
who drag my father
off still shouting,
his gaping pockets
empty, always
empty.

Hexakósioi Hexēkonta Héx

Χξς

In the Book of Revelation,
a beast rises from an abyss
in the sea; seven heads, ten horns
with crowns; on one head a mortal
wound, strangely self-healing—
spawning a cult.

A second beast rises from the earth;
with two horns like a lamb—it speaks
like a dragon, directing
the people of earth to worship
the first beast, persecuting
all who don't.

It is said, although the beast
from the sea is unnamed, it will answer
to the numeric 666. Did François Blanc
know this in the 1860s
when he bargained with the devil
in Monte Carlo for the secrets

of roulette? 666, the triangle
number; *hexakósioi hexēkonta héx;*
the sum of the numbers
on Blanc's roulette wheel;
the Number of the Beast—
the Devil's Number.

The Durban July, 2005

My father's favourite race was the July
when a menagerie of horses ran—
Grey Arrow, Silver Point and The Night Sky.
Irridesence, Eventual, Helmsman.

But, Rabiya, the three-year old dun colt
shattered his cannon in the last hundred:
sounded like a gun, the jockey says. Cold
horse in an outcast state, put down, lies dead.

Something that happens in this kind of sport,
the pundits say so pragmatically…
He was insured—the owner's terse retort.
Such a dampener, the fans moan madly.

The winner was a rank outsider. Sly
bookmakers took fat profits that July.

If only you had said

no, to the fast-rolling dice
on fake green felt;
to the red and black squares
on a spinning wheel;
to the neon lights spiralling
in blackness on a bright sun-yellow day.

If only you had walked
on water, fed loaves
not to the world but to us;
healed, with blue eyes piercing,
not only your body,
but also your mind.

If only you had said
no, to pills in hidden packets,
to casual experiments with ropes
wrought in knots; to differing heights
of chairs and stools; to plots of derelict
land, harbouring abandoned garages.

If only you had said
no, knowing you could walk
away in your rumpled shirt,
shoes time-burnished, hair
flecked grey and white, into open
loving arms that would catch all of you.

An Irreverent Calling

It was the wind that woke me,
buffeting the walls of the house,
bang…bang, bang,
and I walked—no, stumbled—
down the passage, the air dense
in expectation of rain
but there was no culprit
in this half-wakefulness.
Restless in bed again,
I listened
to the inconsolable
bang…bang, bang.
It was only in the morning,
harbouring a headache,
the sound reverberating,
when I heard the news
and wondered if the banging
was never really
a windowpane loose-hinged,
but more a calling, a cymbal,
a clanging announcement
that his time was up.

Dialogue of a Man with His Soul

Death is in my sight. To whom can I speak
of flame and burning fire? Wretched body
a dwelling—together now, let us seek

the gods: Thoth, Re, Isdes—reach, touch my cheek
to judge, listen, defend me as I boldly
declare—death is in my sight; let me speak.

Are you not a man? In sunlight and deep
water lie fish; an offering stone in the bay;
a dwelling place. Together let us seek.

Brother becomes enemy; weak and cheap.
The gentle have perished to embody
death in my sight—to whom can I speak?

Death draws near. Scent of myrrh and blossom; sweet
passing of rain; clearing of sky. A buoy;
a dwelling. Together now, let us seek

morning. *Set mourning aside; I weep*
whether you live or die; I rest, my boy.
Death is in my sight, to whom can I speak?
A dwelling together now let us seek.

Disturbia

In the week before my father died,
we were gripped by an unseen hand—

felt first in the fleeting whine of the eighteen-wheeler
that clipped our car's side mirror,

then in the convulsions of a small body,
as we waited on that gravelled sandy verge

for the child to empty the last of her stomach,
and again, omnipresent at the edges of the lodge,

the wind whistling in the night leaves,
with the howl and yelp of hyena.

I had shivered, wiped the fevered brow of the child,
rinsed her in tepid water, willing the fever to abate,

but, at the doctor's room, I watched the doleful shake
of a head as we were ushered to the hospital

for days, drips and bad dreams;
I remember now, those cruel and furtive fingers

clutching at us as we headed home,
to await that final call—

he had tied a gnarled knot, climbed a crooked
stool, stepped to his freedom—

I had instinctively reached for the child,
was surprised to find her cool to the touch,

serenely sleeping.
I sat still in silence.

II

Inversus

Caretaker! Take care, for we run in straights.
Daily, by night, we walk naked to storm,
some threat of wholesale loss, to ruinous fear.
Gift us with long cloaks & adrenalin.

– John Berryman, 'Eleven Addresses to the Lord'

This Picture Frame: Suburbia

That's the end of my life. The rest is posthumous.
– Ted Hughes

Virginia Woolf filled her overcoat pockets
with stones, and walked into water;
John Berryman threw himself
from the Washington Bridge;
Sylvia Plath tried twice
before she got it right with gas—
the doors to her children's rooms
sealed with tape, towels and cloths;

> Kurt Cobain,
> Anne Sexton,
> Ernest Hemingway,
> Vincent van Gogh—
> even Robin Williams:

but how is it, Dad,
in our suburban house,
amid leavened bread and *labneh*,
two dogs in the yard, *Impatiens*
rooted in flower at the front porch,
that you, like them, became a refugee
seeking this unearthly asylum?

It's Not Like in the Movies

In *Three Billboards Outside Ebbing, Missouri*,
Chief Willoughby leaves notes.
Evocative, sensitive letters read
to the viewer in Woody Harrelson's
deep yet down-to-earth voice:

> *My darling Anne, tonight I have gone
> out to the horses to end it.*

Chief Willoughby's words offer
comfort and advice, explanations
and encouragement, life lessons
for a willing recipient, to be kept folded
in a drawer to be read and re-read.

But our notes were a terse affair—
a line or two of incoherence
scribbled in blue—a child's handwriting—
falling aghast from my fingers,
forsaken on the kitchen floor.

Father at the House of the Dead

It is chill at the mortuary —
cutting sounds clink and echo
as the steel gurney, lopsided,
is wheeled across stone floor.

It was nothing like you read in books,
no peaceful visage, just defiant ash,
a blue line of lips and a sheet
drawn up to under his chin.

What is this clammy strangeness
I witness at the viewing window?
An esoteric strangeness transfixes me
at this Rose Cottage, this Rainbow's End.

And what are those folds, those foreboding
folds of loose and twisted skin?

My Uncle Buried Him

The Maronite Catholic Church stands proud among the offices and highways that surround it. White roses grow in neat lines leading to the entrance and an ornate gold bowl of holy water rests at the entrance where I dip my finger; touch it to my forehead. It is here my father is buried by my uncle. Father James is wearing a white cassock and stole; his hands shake as he rests them on the coffin lid; his voice wavers as his fingers run over the grooves of the pine. He recites the Our Father. He offers the Eucharist. The breeze from that August morning cools our damp faces; we pray and pray; pray for the repose of my Father's soul—secretly pray he will be spared the arm of Minos who condemns such souls to eternity in the second ring of the seventh circle of Hell.

The Ins and Outs of the Inquest Docket

The Krugersdorp police station
is in Commissioner Street—
a prefabricated building prefaced
by a patch of dry sand.
My father's docket can't be located,
only to be dumped, finally, on the table,
the cover dirty and torn.

What are these? I lift
the pile of handwritten notes.

The notes he left, bellows the officer.
Haven't you seen them?

But I only knew my own family's notes.
He concedes and lets me read them
even though they are evidence and he shouldn't.

Why is the inquest taking so long? I mumble.

*The results for the barbiturates
had to be sent to Pretoria.*

Barbiturates?

Quieter now, he spells out how
many of *them* take drugs before—

to help finish off the unspeakable.

Stigmata

At your sister's house
several weeks after the funeral,
we congregate for tea
in apparent conciliation.
A self-appointed head of house,
she is seated at the large wingback chair
while everyone scuttles for teaspoons
and butter amid frazzled nerves.
It was there in the lounge,
apologetically peeling and coring
a large red apple that I ran a knife
clean through the centre of my hand.
Blood spurted from this unholy stigma
sprayed in defiance at your ghost,
dripped onto the tea table,
staining the cake and scones.
It's bad, I whimpered, *it's bad.*
Oh rubbish, said my sister sensibly
as she led me to the bathroom,
my face whitened,
for an overly dramatic mop-up.

Our Bodies, Our Selves

me contra me
– Dante Alighieri, 'Inferno', Canto XIII, 13.72

There is no path in the forest that lies
in the second ring of the seventh circle,
just a labyrinth that leads to self-violent souls.

No foliage there. No fruits. No straight branches,
only curvatures matted and gnarled,
with multitudes of thorns bearing poisons.

Harpies feed on the blackened leaves of these living trees.
Foul creatures, half-animal, half-human: thick-necked
and taloned; bellies fledged with wings.

A wailing emanates from this dark wood,
from all sides, sad plainings; saplings groan,
the winds hiss, splinters draw whispers and blood,

and from each tree-gallow hangs a corpse:
an external husk in a grove of suicide-trees,
grown from a soul-seed, sprouting like spelt.

I Turn a Great Hourglass

Every Tuesday, John Donne imagined he turned a great hourglass;
contemplating life on his last watch; what to do with time left to pass.

Unembellished. Discreet. *Nothing,* he deduced. Unemployed
and shunned following his imprisonment, in this void

he was overtaken by a desire for the liminal next life,
writing a thesis of his morbid condition of strife—

Biathanatos. Suicide, he concludes should be prohibited, save
if committed for God's glory—like Samson who took to the grave

3 000 Philistines and himself; or Saul, who fell on his sword to avoid capture;
or Judas Iscariot who, with a kiss and some silver, hanged himself in rapture

and remorse; and outrageously, he writes, just like Christ,
who chose to emit His own last breath on the cross.

All the psychologists say

suicide is not your fault. You know it's not your fault / as if
it's akin to, say, not turning off the lights when Eskom
demands reduced consumption / or, maybe, flushing
in a water shortage when you know you shouldn't
because you just can't stand the smell / but there
are certain things you cannot come back from / like
there's just no coming back from the sweet smell of
gas, gun casings or, in my case, the end of a noose / so,
the psychologists can say what they want about fault
and guilt and guilt and fault / we who stood over the
body and deciphered the wound / who scrummaged
through frayed notes in broken dockets at police
stations / who stood beneath the bowers in deserted
garages / we all know / we will drive each day / with
a phantom urn resting restlessly on the passenger seat
close beside us.

I Sleep and My Soul Awakens

My father's sister was Dominican.
Stern and learned, she taught perfect English
in a convent. She lived to her eighties,
wrinkled and pale, shrinking in on herself,
to die with the other Sisters standing
vigil in a mandala alongside.
Yesterday, she came to me in a dream,
a halo of light, a background of navy
blue, almost black. Her skin was smooth, youthful,
all peaches and cream, her lips tinged with rose.
She was holding a broken doll: *will you*
take care of this for me? she asked. *Take care*
of this. And in my sleep, I took the doll
from her, clutched it to my breast and wept.

To Will an Apparition

On my walk in the forest this morning,
I willed an apparition. Even just
an optical illusion. No one else.
Only me and the cool stream of water

splashing underfoot. The chirp of wild birds.
I stood on the bridge of dark pine logs bound
by tough wire listening. Watching. Waiting.
Arguing—cajoling—for a vision.

Why can't hope be made visible to those
who will it? Umbra of Earth's deep shadow;
antisolar point, centre of haloes,
sunlight of rainbows, moonlight of glories.

Foolishly squinting into slanted light,
I stooped under the sway of silent trees.

Forty Days

Today I saw a crested barbet.
Chocolate-speckled plumage fluffed,
mustard-red face cocked cheekily to the side,
as he twitched on the edge of an aged acacia tree.

Uncanny really, how often in the weeks after you died,
I saw barbets: me gazing from the bedroom window,
propped up on pillows when the cassias were suddenly
amass with birds, nibbling in a frenzy at the seeds and pods;
then, sitting aimlessly on the patio when from the blue sky
a flock of fifteen or more swooshed into the maples;
and then again, lying in stupor in a lukewarm bath,
when a lone, large, magnificent specimen alighted
in the leopard trees—coal-black eyes, staring right at me.

It is said that after dying, the souls of the dead roam the earth,
returning home to people and places that inhabited their lives.
For forty days, it is said, the soul wanders, seeking out
doorways adorned with the spruce branches of olives,
to rest and take leave.

After forty days, we took the dried olive branches,
the wreaths from over your grave and burnt them.
As the smoke ascended, we said our goodbyes:
no longer come to us, we will come to you.

Zoetrope

For how many years will my blood run cold
as your name and deed are whispered in the chill?
When will your memory in my body unfold?

In restaurants, my future's been foretold
by sages or savants bearing goodwill:
yet, whenever it's said, my blood runs cold.

Running on forest pathways, I must grab hold
of bark or risk my footing to that familiar ill.
When will your memory in my body unfold?

Even the wicked are eventually paroled;
stride out or, broken, limp on up the hill.
For how many years will my blood run cold?

Will months or years, centuries or eons enfold
the cataracts in my eyes—excise and distill
your memory from my body? Or will they unfold

it finally, so I at last can cross the threshold,
don a white cassock, the cross and mitre with will.
For how many years will my blood run cold?
When will your memory in my body unfold?

II

Verbatim

Oil all my turbulence as at Thy dictation
I sweat out my wayward works.
Father Hopkins said the only true literary critic is Christ.
Let me lie down exhausted, content with that.

– John Berryman, 'Eleven Addresses to the Lord'

Dream Sequence

I

In a damp room,
water drips: a hundred jars
stand silent, empty—
all shades of grey,
waiting to be filled.

II

I wait in a weathered rickety
wrought-iron chair,
for drops of water,
pools, lakes, oceans.

In the Misperception of My Life

~ after Adrienne Rich, 'A Clearing in the Imagination'

I

mis
per
cep
tion
mis
taken
mis
prision
mis
con
duct
mis
rep
resent
ation
mis
cons
true
mis
guide

II

in the misperception of my life
i mistake being alive
for wholeness youth for ability
misperceiving
the gravity of the sea
for consistency forgetting
the iceberg
and as i struggle i mis-
perceive dough for bread
neglect the benefits
of the warming oven
in misperception
i run along footpaths
not in the feline
undergrowth of the forest
floor but out in the open
exposed to the elements
gifts upon misprision growing
misprision all about me
delusion rushing upon me
as i wade through its slush
ruthlessly rising to my neck-nape

III

beguile betray cheat confound
deceive delude dupe error
fake fallacy fault falsehood
illude outfox trick unfound

Ars Poetica in *Décima*

In the bounty of life, there lies a lack
among my bookends, pens, pencils and keys.
Up hills at the edge of forests, with ease
I walk between bulrushes and bridge, back
through damp mists rising above streams, cut back
onto soggy footpaths, over smooth stones
and raised roots. Like discarded brittle bones,
there lies a lack that I cannot now write
or reduce with digits to page: a blight
leaching from my pen-tip in monotones.

Pantoum to the Elation of Making

~ found poem after William Kentridge

It's all right. You don't have to run so hard—
there are mountains in the background, trees,
images, memories, waiting to be deployed:
in the elation of making, mistranslation liberates.

Are there mountains in the background, trees,
bits of light joining fragments? Between two worlds,
in the elation of making, mistranslation liberates—
out into the world, back into the body,

bits of light joining fragments. Between two worlds,
there is a mighty Will fighting sleep, circling.
Out into the world, back into the body,
digging with a spade, clods on a coffin.

A mighty Will fighting sleep. Circling
a running zoetrope spiralling the grave
digging with a spade, clods on a coffin,
a metronome, halfway between music and time—

a running zoetrope. Spiralling the grave,
drawing trees on paper from a book of knowledge,
a metronome, halfway between music and time,
to embrace the absent centre. To recharge and renew

by drawing trees from a book of knowledge,
images and memories are deployed
to embrace the absent centre, *se ressourcer.*
It's all right. You don't have to run so hard.

Snowfall

On an indiscriminate Thursday morning,
we stroll along a boardwalk, seaweed
salt-scented in our nostrils, a fine mist
enveloping our limbs, settling in our ears.

The chemo has made your skin pale,
almost translucent, while thin blue veins
wind serpentine from under the watchful
eye of freckles and the thinned skin of eyelids.

Sitting at a coffee shop by the sea,
wrapped in a striped scarf,
you sip berry juice gingerly
through a straw.

As steam rises from my tea,
a sudden gust of wind
whips at us from the ocean.

It was then I witnessed a snowfall—

> hundreds of inch-long strands
> of your fine brown hair, floating about us,
> sprinkling my forearms and thighs
> spiralling onto the table and into the tea.
> *Sorry!* you whisper, *I'm sorry!*
> As you try to brush them off,
> they settle eventually stock-still—

a divination on the floor all about us.

Angelus

Time does not return
– Vincent van Gogh

There were no trains to Auvers-sur-Oise
the day I arrived in Valmondois.
Lost at the station, I crossed the road
through prisms of mist,
to find Claudine, padlocking her gate,
offering to drive me to Auvers.
In her beat-up navy-blue Citroën,
she whizzed through the streets
laughing and chatting.
With the left door jammed then open,
kisses and a farewell hug,
she dropped me at the town hall,
covered today in a canvas scaffolding
—linen cloth lining a corpse—
a halo of mist still swirling about,
and I left wondering:
was she real or just an apparition?

Triptych I

~ *after Vincent van Gogh*

I

Allegory of the Cave

On pilgrimage to the remote *Zweeloo*:
at the horizon between earth and sky,
vistas of corn furrows, moss-covered roofs;
ploughmen, carts and road menders alongside
an avenue of damp autumn poplars;
infinities of heath and a wide road—
a flock of oval muddied shapes jostling
swamp and, now, overcome you in their midst.
Amid this tableau, the sheepfold beckons
as the shepherd leads the procession to
a triangular silhouette of shade:
the gaping hollow of an open cave
is closed by the shepherd and a woman
with a lantern, *lumen infinitum.*

II

Homesick for the Land of Pictures

Michelet, Millet, Shakespeare and Dickens,
were your obsession—immersion a means
of eluding all disillusionment,
musing as you wander, beliefs and loves
elaborated, consolidated,
in drawings and watercolours, etchings
and studies of sowing and ploughing, each
tentatively evoking your homeland.
You, seer, sought an active melancholy,
engrossing yourself in detailed readings:
La Révolution Française, Aeschylus,
Souvestre, *Henry the IV,* the Gospels;
your preference to numb desolation—
the chagrin of your deepening despair.

III

Insight into Exile

I arrived in Auvers in April, with
a grave pewter sky and an icy wind,
a yellow sun burning off the mild mist—
everywhere, almond trees planted in lines,
dark stumps with spring shoots yearning heavenward,
circling the Gothic church and bell-tower,
following me along the Rue des Comptes
as I trace your steps to the *cimetière.*
But, in the courtyard at Auberge Ravoux,
under a warm sun, I must take a breath:
outside the staircase leading to your room,
pilgrims murmuring in hushed tones, I stare
at a singular almond tree, awash
in the tumultuous pink of blossoms.

Triptych II

I

A Caged Bird in Spring

~ after Vincent van Gogh's letter to his brother Theo, July 1880

This spring dawn, a bird wavers, crestfallen
in a cage, waiting, wondering... Sensing
new nests of sticks, soil and feather, brooding,
a hatching of chicks among foliage,
yearning to flock-fly while circling the earth,
on pilgrimage spanning ocean flyways—
yet firmly behind bars, a prisoner.
Immured by poverty, deep malady
and other misfortune, its suffering
wholly unable to render hope, joy
or peace, the caged fledgling, considered now
an idler under a thunderous sky,
seeks moorage: *my God*, it cries, *will it last
long, forever or for eternity?*

II

An Artistic Addiction

~ after Vincent van Gogh's letter to his brother Theo, January 1889

The pearl is the oyster's sickness
– Gustave Flaubert

These pictures are costing me blood and brain:
debt and addiction, body for money,
friends and family are both judge and jury.
Hand clutching a cloth-wrapped ear—a self-inflicted
injury. As wretched hangovers
withdraw then wane, there cannot be any
reckoning for bloodstain. Now how am I
meant to attain amity when visions
only increase my misery? Am I
ruined, insane? Is recompense merely
an illusion? In the midst of this damned
mania, I try to explain: despite
the alcohol, drugs and pain, *I'm sorry—*
these pearls, these pictures, *are* my blood, my brain.

III

In a Mood of Too Much Calm

~ after Vincent van Gogh's letter to his mother and sister, July 1890

Yesterday, in a mood of too much calm,
from purple earth, a tilled and weeded ground,
lost among drifts of grass and pale blossom,
I yielded under stretches of dark skies.
And today I'm harried. Painting in rain,
kneeling in soft clover and fawn pasture,
a train crosses a white road to reveal
my unsteady step. Now, I'm bound to You.
To wield this constant yearning to be whole
and healed, not a blighted burden, confounds
me. On a rickety bed, my bruised mind
a battlefield, I lie spellbound, smoking
my pipe—recalling in this mood of calm
my gun-shot echoing through the wheat field.

Sparrowhawk

Walking in the woodlands,
alongside a stream,
eyes lowered, chin tucked,
I did not see the bird,

just heard the resounding *swoosh*
above my head,
the accompanying *thwack!*
as a fat pigeon plummeted

to the ground, to land at my feet,
stone dead. In bewilderment, I looked
up to see sparrowhawk, imperious,
shaking and Shaka-like,

white feather-coat of underbelly puffed up,
yellow legs gnarled, talons gripping
the underside of the oak branch,
her mandarin eyes alight and staring

right at me: outraged
at the sudden loss of this prize.

Beneath the Albumen, Yolk

~ in memory of Ruth Miller (1919–1969)

Beneath semi-permeable
crystalline shell and two layers
of tough, membranous keratin;
beneath an air cell and layers
of albumen—there rests the yolk:
nutrient rich, spherical,
opaquely anchored to egg-white
by rope-like strands; rich
with vitamins, minerals,
fatty acids, cholesterol;
an incubated embryo,
lavish source of food for my pencil:
Ruth, there you repose, vitelline,
feeding my albuminoid brain—
there you slumber, abundant yolk,
digestible to an infant,
three times as wholesome as egg-white,
astonishingly suspended
in my egg-oval consciousness.

Sending Rain

~ in memory of Chris Mann (1948—2021)

It hadn't rained for months in Makhanda:
only parched earth, the ache of scorched sand, dust,
broken bones—an impossible dryness—
where water was collected in buckets

from the local spring, salvaged from the back
of trucks, or sludge-filled and rendered useless.
While you lay there dying, there were daily
water cuts, sometimes a week at a time.

Yet, on the morning you passed, as dawn broke
and for days after your funeral, mist
coated the earth, rain soaked the sandy soil,

droplets divined in the v's of branches:
like alms offered by Gift of the Givers—
lifegiving boreholes; irrigation; seeds.

Sixth Sense on the *Linga Linga*

~ *Mozambique*

In Inhambane estuary, the late afternoon monsoon
wind blows warm. The dhow creaks, slants
in the waves, lateen sail ballooning, an aerofoil
through the tepid lagoon into the river mouth.

The unassuming helmsman tells how this dhow
belonged to his great-grandfather—his family
have lived comfortably off fish hauled from this craft
for over 100 years. He marks the horizon, points now

to the fading land curved in a natural S,
the water translucent, almost-white, sand visible
on the ocean floor. At the lift of his arm, I stumble
sluggishly to the opposite slate-streaked wooden-slats:

lean back, he says—*lean with the boat's weight;*
my hair is a reckless mob; face inches from the foam.
Hundreds of tiny silver fish race in a sea-womb
beneath me. In impish delight, he tips the boat,

the waves' spray soaking my kikoi,
hands, feet, eyes—my raucous laughter
elicited by this sage with no labour
—an unexpected buoy.

On the Road to Tartarus

~ Mozambique

The journey from the border to Tofo:
an underworld of scrubland in despair;
deserted shacks and abandoned buildings
bombarded by the sun; sand on the road;
no paths in the sand; lament-strewn plastic
in heaps across the road and in the trees;
fire-burned rubble wheezing black-smoke stench;
children running barefoot in shirts or shorts;
and overladen vigilante buses—
one with a goat perched on the roof, roped tight
to the coffin lid, face raised to the sky,
emitting a low, slow howl of terror.

Butanding

~ Mozambique

In Torfino Bay, I swim with a whale shark,
gigantic creature, previously birthed
in my consciousness thanks to *National Geographic*,
now an arm's length from my outreached palm.

Its wide flat head and two small eyes watch me curiously,
brown and cream-speckled, its luminous weight weighs on me.
I lick salt and kelp rind from my lips, my goggles fog,
a cool humming radiates from my ear canals into clumsy limbs.

Buddhists say, when we die, deep attachments and memories
are obstructions. And I'm like a sea horse, tethered to sea grass
on the ocean floor—hastily fluttering my fin, backing away
to halt this striking vision of a life after this one.

Prosōpon

The potter's firm hands
scoop damp-heavy clay
from the shadow earth
and hollow out the dark centre;
her fingers dip in water to shape
and smooth the clay's sharp edges.

Now she patterns the outside,
scrapes out leaves and flowers,
then carefully paints the vase.
To finish, she fires it in the kiln;
places it with grace
on the table in the light.

Threshold

Peru is a country transfixed by doors,
artfully constructed entry-ways, crafted
from rectangular slabs of wood, even
in temperament and stature. Doors of pale yellow ochre,
sage or burgundy, carved in intricate block patterns;
simple slats running perpendicular to the floor;
or whole towns with cerulean-blue doors
—an ancient practice inherited from the conquistadors—
always affixed with a wrought-iron bolt,
almost always never open.

The Incas never used doors, only doorways—
mammoth hexagonal structures of interlocking
masonry with no mortar, a duality of aperture
allowing light in and a daring view out;
trapezoid portals blending geometry
and the natural landscape, embracing the solstices,
the moon, the sun and stars. In holy places,
wooden poles were wedged in doorways denoting
no entry—and removed only when nobles
or the sacred stepped over the threshold.

Reservoir

~ after 'First Lesson' by Philip Booth

In the reservoir,
I recall a dead man's float.
Gliding from one side of circular
cement walls to the other,
where sage water laps,
I salt-lick fingers and ponder—
a dead man's float is face down.
I flip to my back, cool water
seeping to the base of ear canals,
sounds dulled, arms and legs spread-eagled
with the reservoir's circumference—
like Vitruvian Man:
superimposed geometric proportions
of a primordial humanity;
a palm is four fingers,
a foot four palms,
a man twenty-four palms;
as eyes sink to sockets
soaking up an aqua sky,
cirrus clouds and olive branches;
in this cosmography,
in symmetry, I recall—
a dead man's float is face down.

God Presents Herself

~ for Nina and Scott

In the Kruger Park, late afternoon,
on the banks of the Crocodile River,
God presents Herself. As the night moon

rises, a dozen elephant, the matriarch
just metres away, crush and crumple
shrubs and strip the dark bark

from trees; and a baby walks
long-trunked in front of a wide-eyed hare—
here God presents Herself: among the stalks

of elongated green grasses stilled
and the rush of the river over stones,
as the hippo rolls in a wide-mouthed

arc in an oasis of lilac-blossomed
hyacinth, in the black eye of the African
Jacana, God presents Herself.

And then too, at the house,
as I am greeted pale-faced
at the door, your eyes are a luminous

aquamarine—as if hellfire burns
behind each iris; the clarity brought
on by great suffering unloosens,

and on the patio, standing—
not sitting—from the pain—
in the quiet of the house, an unfolding.

The walls are awash with a torrent
of jasmine blossom, the rooms
infused with its heady scent

when we hear the kettle whistle. Wailful.
There too, as we listen to the high-pitched
scream, God presents Herself.

At the Nursery in Rain

I

Today I walk the nursery in rain,
wonder in the damp peace at creation:
tiny flowers of lemon thyme; fine-veined
leaves of scabiosa; silk elation
of bright cotula; artemisia,
its stalks aromatic in the breeze. Rain
falls in a stream; drips a soft aria
onto the pebble floor's patterned terrain.
It patters over the hood that covers
my forehead, hair, ears and face. I startle
as I pull the loaded trolley, smother
my midriff's wound as it pulses; marvel
at water collecting in the splendid
crassula's heart-shaped leaf. It is humid.

II

He is motionless under the bower,
muscular youth. His name tag says, *Jesse.*
I ask, *Can you help me please?* Now louder:
The packed trolley has become so heavy.
Compassion registers in clear brown eyes.
He takes the load, leads me through the entrance
to the car. An eagle in white clouds cries.
We stoop, lift and pack. The rain insistent.

My hands are wet. Water streams down my face,
along the flesh pathway from my jawline,
to neck, along my clavicles. What fate
startles the sun from behind the mountain?
It's a monkey's wedding; a lemon scent.
Under sun, in rain, we unload lament.

On Being Gifted a Life

In a dream, a dervish hands me my eyes:
not the entire eye—only the eyelids.
My hair turns coal, grows lush, falls to my waist.

A hijab swirls loosely, less a bloodied
red, more amber tinged, as if the sun reached
out, startled, to dilute its darkened depths.

The scarf undulates in waves, pendulums
of silk pulsing in the breeze just above
the ochre earth, right to the horizon.

The dervish covers the whites of my eyes
with the skin of my eyelids: I must sew
them together to see in a new light.

Do Not Stride Out to That Vast Lake

~ for Robert

During the horror of your hospital sojourn,
a vast lake appeared for days.
Flat. Dark. Sullen and still it hovered,

its contents murky: parasitic fish;
grim sea urchins; and in the brackish water,
all kinds of dangers lurking —

electric eels, fish with teeth on tongue,
piranhas, vampire fish and giant devil catfish
that leave no remains behind.

Yet, somehow you heard our urging:

remember the warmth of your child's hand,
        remember a cheek on your cheek,
                remember the honey conjured by bees,

and our cries:

                no matter what is inflicted upon you —
                do not stride out to that vast lake.

Anoint the Body

Anoint the body with oil and water,
we were told. Make the sign of the cross. Light a candle.
But the priest said he no longer
anoints the sick in hospital—Covid and all that.
Just too risky. We rolled our eyes.
Even the Priest.

So, every other day, in the ICU,
I anoint your body with holy oil and water.
I, sinner, poor in temperament,
anoint your forehead with oils,
turn your palms to face me,
make the sign of the cross along
the vein of your lifeline, pray for mercy.
I even anoint the machines,
the ventilator, the catheter,
the pipes, tape and tubes—
I sprinkle them all with holy water,
murmur blessings, recite prayers.
Always, always I anoint your sheets,
your metal bed, the foam mattress,
the place where you lie.
I sprinkle water, pretend I am a sage,
rub oil into your temples,
and before I leave, wet your hair with water
curated by others holier than I could ever be.

Finally, I seal the oil and water,
blow out the candle.

Only a miracle can save you now.

Recovery

In *Specimen Days*, Walt Whitman writes of the stroke that rendered him bedridden for years—how in his then half-paralytic body, he regained a life force: *The First Frost; Spring Overtures; A Sun-Bath—Nakedness; The Full-Starr'd Nights*. Page after page, he writes: of midnight migrations of immense flocks of birds; swarms of wild bees in their thousands swelling like a moving cloud, he resting under the wild-cherry enveloped in their drone; of trees, water, grass and sunlight, the moon, and the stars. He renders detailed lists of the names of trees, birdlife, the stars and even the wildflowers; a deep awareness of the nuance of sunlight in every form, the beauty of evening shadows. In *The Lesson of a Tree*, he weighs up the existence of dryads, and extols the power of trees. Sometimes, he wakes at midnight just to watch Venus rise in the blue-black sky and inhale the acoustic air. Frequently, he communes with the invisible physician—a vital presence found in solitary places that imparts a silent medicine to the physical body. Whenever he is able, he hobbles to water, small dams and nearby ponds to watch his favourite kingfishers, to listen to the sounds of nature, to sing robustly out loud, and if his new body allows him, to swim for long stretches in the icy water.

In My Mother's Heart

In my mother's heart rests an abundance of honeysuckle
with the sweet scent of rose water and ripe plums.

There is an open field of long grass with fragrant lilac
wildflowers that rise *en masse* above the sheaves into warm sunlight

My mother's heart renders rare studies—charcoal
drawings in impossible detail of hands folded in a half-circle.

There, each season evolves in a day, the rising sun
alongside the aureole of the moon, the stars in constellation.

In my mother's heart, there are spaces and shadows,
areas of unexpected light that warm to the marrow;

there the sun casts its rays across a lilting stream
revealing grass rising on the far bank, lush and green.

Uncoding Landscape

~ after Seamus Heaney's 'The Peninsula'

Heaney writes when you have nothing more to say
go drive around the peninsula. And, shock-stilled,
I do. Searching the contours for his rocks and logs, fields,
leggy birds, and islands rising out of fog to the bay.

But all I can see is the road before me. A long haul
past twisted chicken-wire fencing and gates, lopsided
and leading me through Chapman's Peak, alongside
cliffs and ravines, where workers in brazen orange overalls

brace canopies onto rocky hillsides, an omen
of falling debris. I search the cirrus skies.
Uncode, Heaney counsels: and my eyes
settle below, on the dense, moon-flat ocean

where, across the bay's expanse, in my far sight,
I spot a speck, a miniature white lighthouse — mature
in its aged loneliness — standing mute; offering in allure,
solace to ships on furious, storm-ridden nights.

Acknowledgements and Permissions

To my family for their support, and to my mother, brother and sister, who walked this path with me, thank you.

I am indebted to Joan Hambidge, my long-time mentor and friend, and to Tony Ullyatt for his assistance and refined suggestions. Thanks also to Sally Ann Murray for her guidance and friendship.

To the many poets falling in the Dryad stable of books, your poetry has inspired and uplifted me and your dedication and commitment to your craft has humbled me.

The striking cover of this collection is thanks to the sublime artistry of Elize de Beer, whom I acknowledge. Thank you also to copy editor, Helen Janisch, for such logical precision in her review of this collection.

Thanks are due to the editors of the following journals and anthologies where versions of some of these poems first appeared: *Stanzas, New Coin, Poetry Potion, Live Canon International Anthology (2017), Atlanta Review, The Sol Plaatje European Union Anthology (2013 and 2019), McGregor Poetry Festival Anthology (2019, 2020 and 2021)* and *I Wish I'd Said (Vol. 3)*.

In particular, I extend thanks to Douglas Reid Skinner and Patricia Schonstein who, since my early days of writing, have published my poems, and continue to do so, in many editions of their respective journals.

Michèle Betty

Notes on Epigraphs and Quotations

Phrases, epigraphs and quotations have been used, sometimes with and sometimes without acknowledgement from the following sources:

All John Berryman epigraphs are from the poem 'Eleven Addresses to the Lord' in *Collected Poems: 1937–1971* by John Berryman (Farrar Strauss and Giroux). Permission to cite John Berryman in epigraphs has been gratefully obtained from Farrar Strauss and Giroux.

Page 5
You've remembered my life for me
In the newspaper article by Jeanne Viall, 'Playful and Poetic' (*Cape Argus*, 21 August 2006), p. 11., Viall recounts how a man approached Denis Hirson following a reading from his famous collection of nostalgic reminiscences, *I Remember King Kong*, and pronounced, 'You've remembered my life for me'.

Pages 7, 8 and 9
Sittoo is Arabic for grandmother and *jiddoo* is Arabic for grandfather.

Page 10
Habibe is Arabic for darling.

Page 12
My bones hold a stillness, the far
Fields melt my heart
Sylvia Plath, 'Sheep in Fog' in *The Collected Poems* (New York: Harper and Row, 1981).

Page 17

If only you knew how fully I myself comprehend the sordidness of my present state.
Fyodor Dostoevsky, *The Gambler* (New York: Random House, Inc., 1992).

Page 18

Hexakósioi Hexēkonta Héx is Greek for six hundred and sixty-six or χξϛ in Greek numerals. The poem is partly based on a rendition of the Book of Revelation (13:11–18) taken from the St James Bible.

Page 22

'Dialogue of a Man with His Soul' creatively interprets text from an essay by the same name, one of the first ever on suicide, composed by an unknown writer in the 12th Dynasty (1937–1759 BC) of the Middle Kingdom in Egypt.

Page 29

That's the end of my life. The rest is posthumous.
Found in Ted Hughes's reply to a condolence letter received following the suicide of Sylvia Plath (Smith College Plath Papers, series 6, Hughes correspondence).

Page 30

Three Billboards Outside Ebbing, Missouri is a 2017 Oscar-winning drama, starring Frances McDormand and Woody Harrelson.

Page 35

me contra me is Italian for 'me against myself' and is from Dante Alighieri's 'Inferno', Canto XIII in *The Divine Comedy of Dante Alighieri* (New York: P. F. Collier & Son Corporation, 1960).

Page 38

The title of the poem, '*I Sleep and my Soul Awakens*', is from Carl Jung's text *Psychology and Alchemy* 2ed (London: Routledge, 1980).

Page 46

Adrienne Rich's essay, 'A Clearing in the Imagination' is in Adrienne Rich, *What is Found There: Notebooks on Poetry and Politics* (New York: W. W. Norton & Company, Inc, 2003, 1993).

Page 49

'Pantoum to the Elation of Making' creatively interprets text from *Footnotes for the Panther: Conversations Between William Kentridge and Denis Hirson* (Johannesburg: Fourthwall Books, 2017).

Page 52

Time does not return
Vincent van Gogh in a letter dated 7 or 8 September 1889 to his brother Theo van Gogh in *The Letters of Vincent van Gogh* (London: Penguin Books Ltd, 1996), p. 459.

Pages 53–58

'Triptych I' and 'Triptych II' are based on a reading of various of the letters of Vincent van Gogh in *The Letters of Vincent van Gogh* (London: Penguin Books Ltd, 1996).

Page 65

Prosōpon, from the ancient Greek, is a theological term used in Christianity as a designation for the concept of a divine person. In English, it is commonly translated as 'person'. In ancient Greek, the term *prosōpon* originally designated one's 'face' or 'mask'. In that sense, it was used in Greek theatre, since actors wore specific masks on stage, in order to reveal their character and emotional state to the audience.

Printed in the United States
by Baker & Taylor Publisher Services